Eggbert was a very fat cat.

Whose owners fed him
this and that.

If he wasn't gorging
himself on food

He'd yowl and meow and
get in a very bad mood.

He'd throw his bowl
around the floor.

As if to say I want
MORE!
MORE!
MORE!

He'd hop atop the kitchen table.

And knock down everything
that he was able

CAT wet Food
CATS
CAT FOOD
CAT FOOD
The family tried to get him to diet

But each time they did, he'd
cause such a big riot!

Until one day, his
attitude changed.

He drank lots of water
and acted all strange.

He couldn't stop drinking,
or peeing and such.

And his owners they noticed,
it was far too, too much

They picked up the phone
and dialed the vet.
Who said, "Bring him right
in; there's no need to fret."

They pulled out the carrier,
which he barely fit in
He had to stand still—that
boy wasn't thin!

The vet looked at Eggbert
and exclaimed with alarm,
That cat is so fat, he's like
a pig on a farm!

He then checked his sugar and
declared with a frown,
He has diabetes and he's got
to slim down!

So Eggbert had to follow a very strict diet,
No more did his family give in to his riots.

They calmed him and combed
him and played with him too.
They used toys to distract him
when he begged for more food.

It was tough there at
first, but in a few days,
He didn't act starved,
too thirsty, or crazed

He lost several pounds and
they sent up a cheer!
He was saved from insulin
shots and the fear.

So when you are tempted to
overfeed your pet,
Just remember old Eggbert
and his trip to the vet.